Vocabulary Wo

British Literature

PEARSON

AGS Globe

Shoreview, Minnesota

ISBN 0-7854-4097-6

A 0 9 8 7 6 5 4 3 2 1

1-800-328-2560
www.agsglobe.com

Table of Contents

Unit 1

Unit 2

Unit 3

Unit 4

Unit 5

Beowulf

Part A Directions The etymology of a word is its history. Use a dictionary to answer these questions. Use complete sentences.

1. What was the meaning of the word *skulk* in its original language?

_____

2. What was the meaning of the Latin word from which *manacle* comes?

_____

3. Look up the etymology of *spurn*. Name a word from another language and its meaning that it resembles.

_____

Part B Directions Match the definition or synonym in Column A with the correct word in Column B. Write the correct letter on each line.

Column A	Column B
_____ **4.** source of ruin	**A** canny
_____ **5.** distress	**B** fens
_____ **6.** clever	**C** bawn
_____ **7.** fearsome	**D** bane
_____ **8.** possessed by a demon	**E** harrowed
_____ **9.** hall	**F** baleful
_____ **10.** deserted	**G** desolate
_____ **11.** uncivilized	**H** heathen
_____ **12.** prevented	**I** bone-lappings
_____ **13.** wet lands	**J** affliction
_____ **14.** joints	**K** demonic
_____ **15.** tormented	**L** forestalled

Beowulf, continued

Part C Directions Match the definition or synonym in Column A with the correct word in Column B. Write the correct letter on each line.

Column A	Column B
_____ **16.** complaining loudly	**A** unremitting
_____ **17.** shameful	**B** lament
_____ **18.** fort	**C** retainer
_____ **19.** attack	**D** keening
_____ **20.** tendons	**E** ignominious
_____ **21.** drew back in fear	**F** sinews
_____ **22.** running	**G** loping
_____ **23.** constant	**H** keep
_____ **24.** wailing	**I** onslaught
_____ **25.** servant	**J** quailed

The Seafarer

Directions Read each clue. Then choose the correct word from the Word Bank to complete the puzzle.

Across	**Down**
1. glowing	**1.** thrived
3. dulled; stained	**2.** seabirds related to gulls
6. pile of material set on fire	**4.** give friendly advice to
7. unfold	**5.** coming to life
9. relative	**8.** grow pale
11. scattering	**10.** guard
13. pure in thought and act	**12.** bitter ill will
14. loneliness	

Word Bank

admonish
blanch
chaste
desolation
fervent
flourished
kinsman
pyre
quickening
rancor
sentinel
strewing
tarnished
terns
unfurl

Sir Patrick Spens, Get Up and Bar the Door

Part A Directions Some words in these ballads are in the Scottish dialect, or the language used in a particular region. Read the lines. Then write the standard English word for each Scottish dialect word in boldface.

1. The **neist** word that Sir Patrick read _____

2. The tear blinded his **e'e.** _____

Part B Directions Write the correct word from the Word Bank to complete each sentence.

3. Sir Patrick Spens is walking on the _____, or beach.

4. Sir Patrick is a skillful, or _____, sailor.

5. The measurement unit used to measure distance across water is the _____.

6. The units used to measure the water's depth are _____.

7. The sailors cry, "_____," because they fear the storm.

8. The seas are rough, or _____.

9. The sailors dreaded, or were _____, to drown in the sea.

10. The ladies wear pretty _____ in their hair.

11. The ballad uses a very old, or _____, dialect.

12. The _____ is the man of the household.

13. The _____ is the woman of the household.

14. The man and woman make a deal, or _____.

15. The man and woman each have much, or _____, stubbornness.

Word Bank
alack
eldern
fathoms
goodman
goodwife
gurly
kames
laith
league
muckle
paction
skeely
strand

The Canterbury Tales

Part A Directions A suffix is a word part added to the end of a word. You can use the knowledge of suffixes to figure out a word's meaning. Identify the meaning of the suffix or suffixes in each of the following words. Then explain what each word means, based on its suffix.

1. courtliness _____

2. blissful _____

Part B Directions Match the definition or synonym in Column A with the correct word in Column B. Write the correct letter on each line.

Column A	Column B
_____ **3.** army on horseback	**A** hallowed
_____ **4.** decorative pin	**B** chivalry
_____ **5.** not religious or cultured	**C** brooch
_____ **6.** clothing and possessions	**D** fustian
_____ **7.** ornamental belt	**E** degree
_____ **8.** one training for military service	**F** cavalry
_____ **9.** causing to exist	**G** array
_____ **10.** the customs of knighthood	**H** baldrick
_____ **11.** social rank	**I** heathen
_____ **12.** sacred	**J** engendering
_____ **13.** long dagger	**K** burnished
_____ **14.** polished	**L** cadet
_____ **15.** cotton and linen fabric	**M** dirk

The Canterbury Tales, continued

Part C Directions Match the definition or synonym in Column A with the correct word in Column B. Write the correct letter on each line.

Column A

Column B

_____ **16.** fought on horseback with lances

_____ **17.** reciting in musical tones

_____ **18.** emotion

_____ **19.** height

_____ **20.** county

_____ **21.** troops moving before an army

_____ **22.** full of concern

_____ **23.** king

_____ **24.** stylish

_____ **25.** unit of length equal to 9 inches

_____ **26.** various

_____ **27.** besides

_____ **28.** three times

_____ **29.** inn

_____ **30.** guard

A sentiment

B span

C withal

D shire

E saucy

F intoning

G thrice

H sundry

I solicitous

J jousted

K van

L ward

M sovereign

N hostelry

O stature

The Book of Margery Kempe

Directions Read each clue. Then choose the correct word
from the Word Bank to complete the puzzle.

Across

1. pantry
6. prevented from doing something
7. town leader
8. an act done to pay for a sin
11. priest who hears confessions
13. tool
14. calmly

Down

2. suffering
3. scold
4. turn away from
5. said false statements about
9. expression
10. pity
11. goodwill
12. cloak

Word Bank

burgess
buttery
charity
compassion
confessor
countenance
forsake
implement
mantle
penance
reprove
restrained
slandered
soberly
tribulation

Le Morte d'Arthur

Part A Directions Some words and phrases in a literary work have figurative instead of literal meanings. Write the answer to these questions. Use complete sentences.

1. In *Le Morte d'Arthur,* Sir Ector says to Arthur, "I was never your father nor of your blood." What is the literal meaning of *blood?*

_____

2. What is the figurative meaning of the word *blood* in the sentence quoted above?

_____

Part B Directions Write the correct word from the Word Bank to complete each sentence.

3. Sir Ector goes to London for business, or his _____.

4. The writing, or _____, on the stone tells who will become king.

5. Arthur is angry, or _____, that he cannot get Sir Kay's sword.

6. Many great barons tried, or _____, to pull out the sword.

7. The Archbishop gives advice, or _____, to the kingdom.

8. Pulling the sword out took no skill, or _____, for Arthur.

9. Arthur expresses sorrow, or _____, that he is not Sir Ector's son.

10. Sir Ector and his wife _____ Arthur as their own son.

11. Arthur is indebted, or _____, to Sir Ector.

12. Arthur was brought to Sir Ector by Merlin's _____.

13. The knights put a tent, or _____, over the sword and the stone.

14. The other knights cannot _____ in getting the sword.

15. Arthur will make Sir Kay the manager, or _____, of his lands.

Word Bank
assayed
beholden
counsel
deliverance
dole
fostered
livelihood
mastery
pavilion
prevail
scripture
seneschal
wroth

The Book of St. Albans

Part A Directions Underline the context clues in the following sentences.
Then define each boldfaced word in your own words.

1. The best, in my simple opinion, is fishing, called **angling,** with a rod and a line and a hook.

_____

2. The salmon is a **noble** fish, but he is difficult to catch.

_____

Part B Directions Match the definition or synonym in Column A with
the correct word in Column B. Write the correct letter
on each line.

	Column A		**Column B**
_____	**3.** weak beer	**A**	dusky
_____	**4.** energetic	**B**	leech
_____	**5.** claim	**C**	alum
_____	**6.** strong liquid used for soap	**D**	onerous
_____	**7.** regret	**E**	verdigris
_____	**8.** tiring	**F**	assertion
_____	**9.** aluminum sulfate	**G**	copperas
_____	**10.** herb used for blue dyes	**H**	lye
_____	**11.** work	**I**	fervent
_____	**12.** poisonous green coloring	**J**	occupation
_____	**13.** likely to argue	**K**	tawny
_____	**14.** doctor	**L**	quarrelsome
_____	**15.** rowdy partying	**M**	treatise
_____	**16.** dark brown	**N**	repentence
_____	**17.** light brown	**O**	russet
_____	**18.** green iron-sulfur compound	**P**	small ale
_____	**19.** reddish brown	**Q**	revelry
_____	**20.** essay	**R**	woad

Sonnet 31

Part A Directions Some English words have changed since the
Renaissance. Write the modern form of each
boldfaced word below.

1. "**thou** feel'st a lover's case"

_____

2. "thou **climb'st** the skies"

_____

3. "Those lovers scorn whom that love **doth** possess?"

_____

Part B Directions Match the definition in Column A with the word in
Column B. Write the correct letter on each line.

	Column A		Column B
_____	**4.** reveals	**A**	wit
_____	**5.** pale	**B**	languish'd
_____	**6.** judged	**C**	deem'd
_____	**7.** reject or dismiss	**D**	wan
_____	**8.** weakened	**E**	virtue
_____	**9.** intelligence	**F**	descries
_____	**10.** goodness	**G**	scorn

On Monsieur's Departure

Part A Directions Antonyms are words with opposite meanings.
Write the antonyms in each line or phrase from
the poem below.

1. "I love and yet am forced to seem to hate."

_____

2. "I freeze and yet am burned."

_____

3. "Or be more cruel, love, and so be kind."

_____

4. "Let me or float or sink."

_____

Part B Directions Match the definition in Column A with the word in
Column B. Write the correct letter on each line.

Column A	Column B
_____ **5.** feel regret or sorrow	**A** discontent
_____ **6.** chatter	**B** passion
_____ **7.** unhappiness	**C** suppressed
_____ **8.** emotion	**D** mute
_____ **9.** put down by force	**E** prate
_____ **10.** silent	**F** rue

Sonnet 75

Part A Directions Some English words have changed since the Renaissance. Write the modern form of each boldfaced word below.

1. "And **eke** my name be wipèd out likewise"

   _____

2. "Vain man (said she) that **dost** in vain assay"

   _____

3. "Not so (**quod** I)"

   _____

Part B Directions Complete each sentence with the correct word or phrase from the Word Bank.

4. The man and woman strolled along the _____.

5. The man tried _____ to keep the waves from the name written in the sand.

6. Poets often _____ to make their words last forever.

7. The woman thought the man was _____ to think he could write immortal words.

8. Great writing is a way to _____, or give lasting fame, to a person.

9. The poet hoped his poem would _____ his love for the woman.

10. The poet said only things lacking great qualities, or _____ things, would die in dust.

Word Bank
assay
baser
eternise
immortalise
in vain
strand
vain

Of Studies

Directions Read each clue. Then choose the correct word from the Word Bank to complete the puzzle.

Across

1. careful ordering
3. debate
5. stoppage
7. formal discussing of views
10. remedy
11. overwhelm in argument
12. laziness

Down

1. more common
2. posing; pretending
3. dislike
4. rational talk
6. trimming
8. assignment
9. pieces of advice
10. the art of speaking or writing

Word Bank

affectation
conference
confute
contemn
contend
counsels
deputy
discourse
marshalling
meaner
proyning
receipt
rhetoric
sloth
stond

Pastoral Poems

Part A Directions The etymology of a word is its history. Use a dictionary to answer the questions about etymology below.

1. From what Latin word does *kirtle* come? What does the Latin word mean?

_____

2. From which Old French word does the word *folly* come? What does the Old French word mean?

_____

Part B Directions Write the correct word from the Word Bank to complete each sentence.

3. The passionate shepherd imagined _____ sung by birds.

4. He pictured many _____ dancing for his love each day.

5. The shepherd wanted to _____, or experience, country pleasures.

6. He described spring delights such as roses and leaves from the _____.

Word Bank
dumb
gall
madrigals
myrtle
prove
reckoning
swains
wanton

7. The shepherd's love knew that when spring ended the birds would become _____, or silent.

8. She knew the lush, or _____, fields would turn wintry.

9. She described the _____, or bitterness, that would follow a lovely spring.

10. The nymph's poem is a summing up, or _____, of the reality of love.

Sonnet 116, Sonnet 130

Part A Directions   You can use context clues to figure out the meanings of some unfamiliar words. They are often implied through contrasts, descriptions, or explanations. Underline the context clues in the following sentences. Then define each boldfaced word in your own words.

1. "[Love] is an ever-fixèd mark,/That looks on **tempests** and is never shaken."

_____

2. "I grant I never saw a goddess go,—/My mistress, when she walks, **treads** on the ground."

_____

Part B Directions   Match the definition in Column A with the word in Column B. Write the correct letter on each line.

Column A	Column B
_____ **3.** colored grayish red	**A** bark
_____ **4.** circle; boundary	**B** belied
_____ **5.** obstacles	**C** compass
_____ **6.** curved blade on a wooden handle	**D** damask'd
_____ **7.** gives off	**E** dun
_____ **8.** gave a false impression of	**F** impediments
_____ **9.** boat	**G** reeks
_____ **10.** dull, drab	**H** sickle

Hamlet

Part A Directions The meanings of some English words have changed
since the Renaissance. Write the meaning of each
boldfaced word as it was used in *Hamlet.* Then write
the most common meaning of the word today.

1. ". . . That he, as 'twere by accident, may here/**Affront** Ophelia."

_____

2. "The harlot's cheek . . . is not more ugly . . . than is my deed to my most **painted** word."

_____

3. "I am myself **indifferent** honest."

_____

Part B Directions Match the definition in Column A with the word in
Column B. Write the correct letter on each line.

Column A

_____ **4.** burdens

_____ **5.** violent; disorderly

_____ **6.** spies

_____ **7.** madness

_____ **8.** face; mask

_____ **9.** very religious

_____ **10.** insulting behavior

_____ **11.** completion; end

_____ **12.** disturbing

_____ **13.** sickness; suffering

_____ **14.** dagger

_____ **15.** normal, usual

Column B

A affliction

B bodkin

C consummation

D contumely

E espials

F fardels

G grating

H lunacy

I pious

J turbulent

K visage

L wonted

Hamlet, continued

Part C Directions Read each clue. Then choose the correct word
from the Word Bank to complete the puzzle.

Across

1. interaction
4. outcome
5. importance
7. frame of mind
9. walk unnaturally
12. beg
14. kick out
16. talk in a false way
17. determination to act
18. person who keeps a brothel

Down

1. insults
2. madness
3. prayers
6. a place where one will not be tempted
8. payments to a king
10. have some trace
11. become
13. ruined
15. height
17. direct

Word Bank	
affections	lisp
amble	moment
bawd	nunnery
blasted	orisons
calumny	pitch
commerce	relish
disclose	resolution
ecstasy	round
entreat	tribute
expel	wax

Psalm 23

Part A Directions Figurative language uses words in a vivid way that is not to be taken literally. Explain the literal meaning of each figurative phrase below.

1. "The LORD is my shepherd."

_____

2. "He maketh me to lie down in green pastures."

_____

3. "Thy rod and thy staff they comfort me."

_____

4. "My cup runneth over."

_____

5. "I will dwell in the house of the LORD for ever."

_____

Part B Directions Write the meaning of each word below in your own words.

6. rod _____

7. staff _____

8. anointest _____

Part C Directions Use each word in a sentence.

9. rod _____

10. staff _____

Valediction, Forbidding Mourning

Part A Directions Prefixes and suffixes add to the meaning of words. Underline each suffix in each word below. Look up the meaning of each suffix in a dictionary and write it below. Then write the meaning of each word based on your knowledge of the base word and suffix.

1. careless

_____

2. expansion

_____

3. firmness

_____

Part B Directions Complete each sentence with the correct word from the Word Bank.

4. The woman fears her husband's trip will create a
_____ between the couple.

5. The poet says his love is not like that of ordinary,
or _____, lovers.

6. He does not want his wife to tell the general mass of people,
or _____, about their love.

7. The poet compares _____, or tremors,
of the earth to movements in the universe.

8. The poet considers talking about their love a _____,
or a dishonoring.

9. One foot of a compass follows the other _____,
or at an angle.

10. The man and woman are so close that they are _____
of their love.

Word Bank
breach
inter-assurèd
laity
obliquely
profanation
sublunary
trepidations

Still to Be Neat, To Celia

Part A Directions Figurative language uses words in a vivid way that is not to be taken literally. Tell whether the examples below are literal or if they include figurative language. Then explain the literal meaning of each figurative phrase.

1. "Such sweet neglect more taketh me
   Than all th' adulteries of art;
   They strike mine eyes, but not my heart."

   _____

2. "Give me a look, give me a face
   That makes simplicity a grace"

   _____

3. "The thirst that from the soul doth rise
   Doth ask a drink divine"

   _____

Part B Directions Complete each sentence with the correct word from the Word Bank.

4. It is _____ that many women use makeup and perfume.

5. Do you consider these _____, or falseness?

6. Many people prefer using makeup instead of the _____ of their appearance.

7. The poet wants to _____ himself to Celia.

8. He wants the two of them to _____ a cup of wine.

9. The drink he wants is _____, or the wine of the gods.

10. The speaker hopes their love, like the wreath, will stay fresh and not become _____.

Word Bank
adulteries
nectar
neglect
pledge
presumed
sup
wither'd

To the Virgins, to Make Much of Time

Part A Directions A word's connotation is the implied meaning over and beyond its dictionary meaning. For example, the word *home* has a positive connotation of love and warmth. In your own words, describe the connotation of each boldfaced word below. Tell whether it is positive or negative.

1. "Gather ye **rosebuds** while ye may."

_____

2. "That age is best which is the first,/When **youth** and blood are warmer."

_____

3. "For having lost but once your **prime** . . ."

_____

4. "You may for ever **tarry.**"

_____

Part B Directions Write the meaning of each word below in your own words.

5. coy _____

6. succeed _____

7. tarry _____

Part C Directions Use each word in a sentence.

8. succeed _____

9. tarry _____

10. coy _____

To Lucasta, on Going to the Wars

Part A Directions Breaking a word apart into its base, prefixes, and suffixes can help you figure out its meaning. Underline each prefix or suffix in each word below. Look up the meaning of each prefix or suffix in a dictionary and write it below. Then write the meaning of each word based on your knowledge of the base word and suffix.

1. unkind

_____

2. faithful

_____

3. disquiet

_____

4. adorable

_____

Part B Directions Write the meaning of each word below in your own words.

5. chaste _____

6. inconstancy _____

7. nunnery _____

Part C Directions Use each word in a sentence.

8. inconstancy _____

9. nunnery _____

10. chaste _____

To His Coy Mistress

Part A Directions An allusion is a detail that refers to religion, history, or another work of literature. Briefly explain each allusion below from the poem. Then tell how it adds to the richness of the poem.

1. "Thou by the Indian Ganges' side/Shouldst rubies find."

_____

2. "I by the tide/Of Humber would complain."

_____

3. "I would/Love you ten years before the Flood."

_____

Part B Directions Match the definition in Column A with the word in Column B. Write the correct letter on each line.

Column A	Column B
_____ **4.** lives in the body	**A** amorous
_____ **5.** shyness	**B** conversion
_____ **6.** tomb	**C** coyness
_____ **7.** passionate	**D** slow-chapt
_____ **8.** slow-moving	**E** transpires
_____ **9.** a change from one religion to another	**F** vault
_____ **10.** slowly devouring	**G** vegetable

Paradise Lost

Part A Directions The etymology of a word is its history. Use a dictionary
to answer the questions about etymology below.

1. What is the meaning of the Latin word from which *adamantine* comes?

_____

2. What is the meaning of the Greek word from which *myriad* comes?

_____

3. The word *dire* comes from the Latin word *dirus,* which is related to a Greek word.
What is the Greek word and its meaning?

_____

Part B Directions Write the correct word from the Word Bank to
complete each sentence.

Word Bank
affliction
baleful
confounded
doleful
ethereal
guile
impious
ken
obdurate
penal
perdition
tempestuous

4. The Serpent used trickiness, or _____, to deceive Eve.

5. Satan was an evil, or _____, being.

6. Satan waged an unholy, or _____, war against God.

7. God threw Satan out of his _____, or heavenly,
surroundings.

8. One of Satan's faults was his _____, or stubborn, pride.

9. God sentenced Satan to _____, or eternal hell.

10. Satan felt frustrated, or _____, by his fate.

11. In hell, Satan is surrounded by _____, or suffering.

12. A dungeon is all that is within Satan's _____, or sight.

13. His surroundings are stormy, or _____.

14. Satan is a miserable, _____ resident of hell.

15. Milton describes God's punishing, or _____, fire.

Paradise Lost, continued

Part C Directions Match the definition in Column A with the word
or phrase in Column B. Write the correct letter on
each line.

Column A	Column B
_____ **16.** powerful	**A** apostate
_____ **17.** bragging	**B** contention
_____ **18.** deep disgrace	**C** deify
_____ **19.** magnificent	**D** durst
_____ **20.** dared	**E** ignominy
_____ **21.** worship	**F** mutual league
_____ **22.** partnership	**G** potent
_____ **23.** abandoning a previous loyalty	**H** suppliant
_____ **24.** humbly begging	**I** transcendent
_____ **25.** rivalry; competition	**J** vaunting

Eve's Apology in Defense of Women

Part A Directions Sometimes words are used in a figurative instead of a literal way. Underline the word or words below that are used in a figurative way.

1. "And then to lay the fault on Patience' back,
   That we (poor women) must endure it all."

   _____

2. "... which, if thy heart relent,
   Why wilt thou be a reprobate with Saul
   To seek the death of him that is so good, ..."

   _____

Part B Directions Circle the letter of the answer that correctly completes each sentence.

3. A person with no insight or understanding is ____.
   A reprobate   **B** undiscerning   **C** strait   **D** bereaved

4. Amelia Lanier believed women should not suffer cruelty, or ____.
   A indiscretion   **B** sovereignty   **C** vengeance   **D** tyranny

5. To scold someone is to ____ him or her.
   A reprove   **B** breach   **C** imbrue   **D** stay

6. Lanier begged Pontius Pilate not to be cruel, or ____.
   A undiscerning   **B** reprobate   **C** barbarous   **D** strait

7. Lanier thought women were deprived, or ____, of respect.
   A bereaved   **B** reproved   **C** condescended   **D** alleged

8. A corrupt person is a ____.
   A barbarous   **B** vengeance   **C** tyranny   **D** reprobate

9. A wrongdoing is a(n) ____.
   A reprove   **B** affliction   **C** indiscretion   **D** malice

Eve's Apology in Defense of Women, continued

10. Eve brought forward, or ____, God's authority.
 A alleged **B** bereaved **C** condescended **D** imbrued

11. Lanier believed men should not have supreme control, or ____.
 A indiscretion **B** tyranny **C** vengeance **D** sovereignty

12. People may seek punishment, or ____, in return for a wrong.
 A tyranny **B** vengeance **C** malice **D** sovereignty

13. A violation of a law is a ____.
 A reprove **B** strait **C** breach **D** stay

14. Lanier says that Pontius Pilate's sin passes, or ____, all others.
 A breaches **B** bereaves **C** stays **D** surmounts

15. A person who wishes to hurt other people or cause suffering has ____.
 A malice **B** imbrue **C** vengeance **D** indiscretion

Gulliver's Travels

Part A Directions Some words have more than one meaning. Write the definition of each boldfaced word below as it is used in the selection. Then write a common definition of the word today.

1. ". . . one was a Page, who held up his **Train** . . ."

   _____

   _____

2. "There were Shoulders, Legs, and Loins shaped like those of Mutton, and very well **dressed** . . ."

   _____

   _____

Part B Directions Match the definition in Column A with the word in Column B. Write the correct letter on each line.

Column A	Column B
_____ 3. dealt with	**A** buff jerkin
_____ 4. a case for holding arrows	**B** prudent
_____ 5. flight of missiles	**C** volly
_____ 6. twist violently	**D** ligatures
_____ 7. formal speech	**E** conjectured
_____ 8. leather jacket	**F** disposed
_____ 9. bindings	**G** oration
_____ 10. supposed	**H** wrench
_____ 11. shot	**I** discharged
_____ 12. wise	**J** quiver

Gulliver's Travels, continued

Part C Directions Write the correct word from the Word Bank
to complete each sentence.

| **Word Bank** |
| dexterity |
| diminutive |
| disapprobation |
| draught |
| forbear |
| hogsheads |
| ingenious |
| intrepidity |
| laden |
| mutton |
| orator |
| prodigious |
| submissive |

13. Gulliver was surprised at how small, or _____,
the people of Lilliput were.

14. He felt _____ next to them.

15. He was _____ to them, even though
he was much larger.

16. He heard a(n) _____ give a powerful speech.

17. Gulliver was so hungry that he could not _____
asking for food.

18. The Lilliputians went to Gulliver _____
with baskets of food.

19. They brought him wine in _____.

20. He ate meat that was similar to _____.

21. He drank an entire container of wine in a single
_____.

22. Gulliver found the Lilliputians _____,
or clever.

23. They also showed skill, or _____,
in feeding him.

24. Gulliver was impressed by their _____,
or lack of fear.

25. The person of high rank responded with _____
to Gulliver's request to be set free.

A Letter to Her Daughter

Part A Directions The suffixes *-ist, -er, -an,* and *-ian* can be used to describe a person who performs a certain action. Use a dictionary to identify and define the suffix in each word below. Then define the word based on your knowledge of the suffix.

1. arithmetician

_____

2. linguist

_____

3. transcriber

_____

Part B Directions Match the definition in Column A with the word in Column B. Write the correct letter on each line.

	Column A		Column B
_____	**4.** denial of a passion	**A**	brutes
_____	**5.** unmarried	**B**	edifices
_____	**6.** spoiled	**C**	unintelligible
_____	**7.** having intellectual insight	**D**	divine
_____	**8.** firmly established	**E**	mortification
_____	**9.** buildings	**F**	incapacitating
_____	**10.** animals	**G**	virgin
_____	**11.** clergyman	**H**	profound
_____	**12.** disabling	**I**	corrupted
_____	**13.** not capable of being understood	**J**	inveterate

A Letter to Her Daughter, continued

Part C Directions Write the correct word from the Word Bank
to complete each sentence.

14. Montagu wrote a long _____
    to her daughter.

15. She expresses _____, or care,
    for her granddaughter.

16. She hopes her granddaughter will be _____
    in much learning.

17. Montagu hopes the girl has a(n) _____
    for learning.

18. Learning new things _____ her,
    or filled her with pride.

19. She _____, or regretted, that she had
    gained literary fame.

20. Women of Montagu's time often studied in
    _____, with no one else nearby.

21. Montagu writes that people who enjoy reading do not need other,
    more expensive _____.

22. Montagu occasionally makes a(n) _____,
    or comment off the subject, in her letter.

23. Montagu expresses her opinions about
    _____, or marriage.

24. She is not sure if her granddaughter should
    _____ into marriage.

25. Deciding whether to marry is a(n) _____
    decision for Montagu's granddaughter.

Word Bank
digression
diversions
elated
epistle
inclination
indulged
inevitable
lamented
matrimony
solicitude
solitude
venture

A Journal of the Plague Year

Part A Directions A word's connotation is the implied meaning over and beyond its dictionary meaning. For example, the word *home* has a positive connotation of love and warmth. In your own words, describe the connotation of each boldfaced word below. Tell whether it is positive or negative.

1. "We had no such thing as printed newspapers in those days to spread **rumours** and reports of things . . ."

_____

_____

2. ". . . abundance of poor despairing creatures . . . wandered away into the fields and Woods, and into secret uncouth places almost anywhere, to **creep** into a bush or hedge and die."

_____

_____

Part B Directions Write the correct word from the Word Bank to complete each sentence.

3. The people of London had much _____, or discussion, about the plague.

4. The _____ rate from the plague was high.

5. People of the time were terrified of this disease, or _____.

6. The people who _____ together in the poor parts of the city often caught the disease.

7. People from these _____ had few ways to deal with the disease.

8. On the other hand, wealthy people, or _____, could often leave town.

9. Sick people were _____ wherever they got sick so that they would not spread the disease.

10. A doctor, or _____, could not cure the disease.

Word Bank
chirurgeon
discourse
distemper
gentry
mortality
parishes
sequestered
thronged

A Journal of the Plague Year, continued

Part C Directions Match the definition in Column A with the word in
Column B. Write the correct letter on each line.

Column A	Column B
_____ **11.** done without	**A** fleet
_____ **12.** countless	**B** compass
_____ **13.** importance	**C** preservatives
_____ **14.** boundary	**D** melancholy
_____ **15.** group of ships	**E** innumerable
_____ **16.** depressing	**F** invention
_____ **17.** allowed	**G** foreborne
_____ **18.** rugged	**H** moment
_____ **19.** things used to protect against decay	**I** uncouth
_____ **20.** product of imagination	**J** suffered

An Essay on Man

Directions Read each clue. Then choose the correct word
from the Word Bank to complete the puzzle.

Across

1. seeking to reach a goal
5. moons
7. person in a leading position
11. moves toward
13. horse
14. area or range

Down

1. silver or white
2. overstepping proper bounds
3. delight
4. god
6. position
8. consistent; understandable
9. spread throughout every part
10. engage the whole attention of
12. reverse

Word Bank
argent
aspiring
coherent
deity
engross
gust
invert
pervading
presumptuous
principal
satellites
sphere
station
steed
verges

Elegy Written in a Country Churchyard

Part A Directions Prefixes can help you figure out the meanings of unfamiliar words. Identify the prefix in each word below. Use a dictionary to define the prefix and the root word. Then define the word.

1. inevitable

_____

2. ingenuous

_____

3. circumscribe

_____

4. recompense

_____

Part B Directions Match the definition in Column A with the word in Column B. Write the correct letter on each line.

	Column A		Column B
_____	**5.** perhaps	**A**	impute
_____	**6.** merrily	**B**	clarion
_____	**7.** stringed instrument	**C**	heraldry
_____	**8.** disturb	**D**	rill
_____	**9.** small brook	**E**	molest
_____	**10.** ballad	**F**	wonted
_____	**11.** usual	**G**	jocund
_____	**12.** a loud, clear trumpet	**H**	lay
_____	**13.** blame	**I**	haply
_____	**14.** family history	**J**	lyre

Elegy Written in a Country Churchyard, continued

Part C Directions Write the correct word from the Word Bank
to complete each sentence.

15. The poet is walking thoughtfully through a rural
    _____.

16. The poet is far from the _____,
    or frenzied, crowds of the city.

17. He hears the _____ ring.

18. The poet walks through the _____, or field.

19. He sees a _____, or rural, graveyard.

20. He thinks about the villagers who are _____
    in their graves.

21. He thinks about the _____, or simple,
    people buried there.

22. Many of the people are penniless; they live in
    _____.

23. Poverty can make even _____ people unhappy.

24. The people are _____, or isolated
    in their small village.

25. The poet knows that _____ men
    who could have been heroes are buried there.

26. He imagines the _____ sung at their funerals.

27. The poet is a(n) _____, or philosopher.

28. He imagines running into a(n) _____,
    or shepherd.

29. The imagined shepherd recites the _____,
    or chronicles, of another young man.

30. The young man's epitaph mentions the generosity, or
    _____ , that the young man had in life.

Word Bank
annals
bounty
curfew
dauntless
dirges
genial
glebe
hamlet
madding
moralist
mould'ring
penury
rude
rustic
sequester'd
swain

Dictionary of the English Language

Part A Directions Many English words are based on Greek and Latin roots. Find the meaning of the Greek or Latin root in each word below. Then write the definition of the word based on its root.

1. malignant

_____

2. affinity

_____

3. confounded

_____

Part B Directions Write the correct word from the Word Bank to complete each sentence.

4. Johnson expected little _____ from critics for his dictionary.

5. The _____ of a word is an interesting part of its dictionary listing.

6. Johnson had several workers who helped _____ the work on his dictionary.

7. The dictionary details the _____, or meaning, of words.

8. The work on Johnson's dictionary was _____ because it was a huge job.

9. The dictionary is a book of _____, or collected, knowledge.

10. Johnson's dictionary included _____ words, which we sometimes call *jargon*.

Word Bank
aggregated
cant
etymology
facilitate
protracted
recompence
signification

Dictionary of the English Language, continued

Part C Directions Match the definition in Column A with the word
in Column B. Write the correct letter on each line.

Column A	Column B

_____ **11.** eager   **A** caprices

_____ **12.** cut with blows of a heavy tool   **B** revelation

_____ **13.** ranking   **C** solicitous

_____ **14.** sudden understanding   **D** delusive
of truth or reality

E hierarchy

_____ **15.** false

F hewn

_____ **16.** insulting treatment   **G** insolence

_____ **17.** approves   **H** avail

_____ **18.** sudden whims   **I** countenances

_____ **19.** failure   **J** miscarriage

_____ **20.** help

The Life of Samuel Johnson

Part A Directions You can use context clues to figure out the meanings of some unfamiliar words. They are often implied through contrasts, descriptions, or explanations. Underline the context clues in the following sentences. Then define each boldfaced word in your own words.

1. ". . . the books themselves, in which he had marked the passages with a black-lead pencil, the traces of which could easily be **effaced**."

_____

2. "I never knew any man who **relished** good eating more than he did."

_____

3. "He used to **descant** critically on the dishes which had been at table where he had dined or supped . . ."

_____

Part B Directions Circle the letter of the answer that correctly completes each sentence.

4. The histories of words are ____.
   A significations   **B** etymologies   **C** copyists   **D** proverbs

5. Writing a dictionary of the entire English language is a(n) ____ job.
   A prodigious   **B** temperate   **C** abstemious   **D** undaunted

6. A person who eats and drinks a moderate amount is ____.
   A abstemious   **B** rivetted   **C** prodigious   **D** temperate

7. A difficult task is ____ .
   A prodigious   **B** temperate   **C** arduous   **D** effaced

8. A person who appreciates subtle details has ____.
   A etymologies   **B** descant   **C** moderation   **D** discernment

The Life of Samuel Johnson, continued

9. A person with his eyes firmly on the TV screen can be said to be ____.
   A temperate   **B** rivetted   **C** abstemious   **D** effaced

10. Biographers often want to write about a(n) ____ character.
   A temperate   **B** noble   **C** abstemious   **D** effaced

11. If you refrained from eating and drinking, you would be ____.
   A rivetted   **B** effaced   **C** temperate   **D** abstemious

12. As friends, Boswell and Johnson probably ____ together often.
   A relished   **B** supped   **C** undaunted   **D** effaced

13. Johnson was assisted in writing the dictionary by several ____.
   A significations   **B** counting-houses   **C** copyists   **D** nobles

14. If you are not discouraged by a setback, you are ____.
   A undaunted   **B** arduous   **C** abstemious   **D** prodigious

15. To write the dictionary, Johnson had to know various ____ of words.
   A discernment   **B** proverbs   **C** descant   **D** significations

A Vindication of the Rights of Woman

Part A Directions Some English words come from words in other
languages. Use a dictionary to help you answer
the following questions.

1. From what French word does *homage* come? What does it mean?

_____

_____

2. Wollstonecraft compares the "flaunting leaves" of a plant to women. From what language or group
of languages does *flaunt* come? What was its meaning? What is its meaning today?

_____

_____

Part B Directions Match the definition in Column A with the word in
Column B. Write the correct letter on each line.

Column A	Column B
_____ **3.** those who create offspring	**A** specious
_____ **4.** having a demanding attitude	**B** abrogated
_____ **5.** law or custom	**C** misconstruction
_____ **6.** lack of respect	**D** propagators
_____ **7.** openness; responsiveness	**E** contempt
_____ **8.** made invalid	**F** perpetual
_____ **9.** having a false look of truth	**G** prerogative
_____ **10.** misunderstanding	**H** fastidious
_____ **11.** going on forever	**I** constitution
_____ **12.** exclusive right, power, or privilege	**J** susceptibility

A Vindication of the Rights of Woman, continued

Part C Directions Write the correct word from the Word Bank
to complete each sentence.

Word Bank
abhorrence
affectations
agitate
apathy
condescend
conspicuous
deplore
eradicate
feign
frivolous
indignation
inveigh
prevalent

13. Mary Wollstonecraft wrote her essay to _____
the poor position of women in society.

14. She felt that women's lack of power was obvious,
or _____ .

15. Wollstonecraft had a(n) _____, or hatred,
for the way women of her time were educated.

16. She did not like the way men _____ to women.

17. The _____, or widespread, attitude was that
a woman's goal should be to get married.

18. Wollstonecraft knew that women had many
_____, or artificial behaviors.

19. Women of her time would often _____
weakness to attract men.

20. They were happy to spend their time in _____
pursuits instead of using their minds.

21. The behavior of both men and women filled Wollstonecraft with
_____ .

22. Wollstonecraft had to fight against women's
_____, or lack of interest, in their situation.

23. She hoped to _____ society
to change it.

24. Wollstonecraft used her essay to _____
against society.

25. It would take many more years to _____
the unfair laws against women.

A Vindication of the Rights of Woman, continued

Part D Directions Match the definition in Column A with the word
in Column B. Write the correct letter on each line.

Column A	Column B
_____ **26.** lazily	**A** vanities
_____ **27.** name or title	**B** libertine
_____ **28.** abusive words or phrases	**C** appellation
_____ **29.** vanishing quickly	**D** gallantry
_____ **30.** not direct	**E** epithets
_____ **31.** lack of energy	**F** inculcated
_____ **32.** things that are empty or valueless	**G** evanescent
	H supinely
_____ **33.** romantic attention	**I** languor
_____ **34.** taught by repeated teaching	**J** oblique
_____ **35.** not held back by morals	

Lines Composed a Few Miles Above Tintern Abbey

Part A Directions Write the answer to these questions. Use complete
sentences.

1. What word is an antonym for *tranquil*? Explain why you chose it.

   _____

2. Is *gloomy* a synonym for *genial*? Explain why or why not.

   _____

Part B Directions Write the correct word from the Word Bank
to complete each sentence.

Word Bank
cataract
harmony
pastoral
perceive
perplexity
raptures
recompense
solitary
subdue
sublime
trivial
unintelligible
vagrant

3. The calculus book was _____ to me.

4. His beautifully _____ singing brought
   tears of joy to my eyes.

5. Maria was in _____ when she heard
   that she had won a trip she had dreamed of all her life.

6. By watching him closely, I could _____
   that he was nervous.

7. Peace and _____ are better than quarreling.

8. Help me _____ this energetic dog.

9. Sam lived a _____ life as he hiked
   in the mountains for the summer.

10. Money is not good _____ for loss of life.

11. The _____ painting showed pleasant fields.

12. This magazine often has _____ articles
    instead of real news.

13. We felt the wet spray from the roaring _____.

14. A lighthouse keeper lives a _____ life.

15. His rambling answer left me in _____..

Lines Composed a Few Miles Above Tintern Abbey, continued

Part C Directions Circle the letter of the answer that correctly completes
each sentence.

16. The _____ of the ruined castle took many years to complete.
    A zeal   **B** ecstasies   **C** exhortations   **D** restoration

17. I thought Hannah would be bored, but she showed great _____ to learn.
    A roe   **B** zeal   **C** secluded   **D** intercourse

18. I like to read in a quiet, _____ part of my backyard where no one else comes.
    A secluded   **B** zeal   **C** sportive   **D** exhortations

19. The students were in _____ of delight when they heard they could go home early.
    A restoration   **B** zeal   **C** ecstasies   **D** secluded

20. In spite of Mom's _____ to stay home, we went to the party.
    A ecstasies   **B** exhortations   **C** recognitions   **D** restoration

Part D Directions Match the definition in Column A with the correct word
in Column B. Write the correct letter on each line.

Column A	Column B
_____ 21. playful or reckless	**A** chasten
_____ 22. belonging to one who lives alone	**B** corporeal
_____ 23. of the physical body	**C** hermit's
_____ 24. related to wooded areas	**D** impels
_____ 25. figuring something out	**E** intercourse
_____ 26. a type of British deer	**F** interfused
_____ 27. punish	**G** recognitions
_____ 28. blended together	**H** roe
_____ 29. urges forward	**I** sportive
_____ 30. dealings between persons or groups	**J** sylvan

Grasmere Journals

Part A Directions Write the answer to these questions. Use complete sentences.

1. Why does Dorothy Wordsworth see so many flowers on her walk?

_____

2. Dorothy Wordsworth mentions seeing birches, primroses, woodsorrel, anemone, and daffodils. Which of these plants is different from the others? Explain why.

_____

Part B Directions Circle the letter of the answer that correctly completes each sentence.

3. A mass of bright yellow ____ catches Dorothy Wordsworth's eye.
   A stragglers   **B** birches   **C** daffodils   **D** miscellany

4. She also sees ____, which are related to buttercups.
   A primroses   **B** violets   **C** woodsorrel   **D** anemone

5. Wordsworth says that the flowers "seemed as if they verily laughed."
   Today we would more likely say that they ____ seemed to laugh.
   A really   **B** sometimes   **C** almost   **D** never

6. William Wordsworth picks up a miscellany, or a ____, after supper.
   A collection of writings   **C** local newspaper
   B long novel   **D** warm sweater

7. Dorothy Wordsworth calls some of the flowers stragglers because they are ____.
   A not yet in bloom   **C** much smaller than the others
   B separated from the other flowers   **D** struggling to stand up straight

8. If you saw an anemone in the woods, you might ____.
   A call for help   **B** stoop to smell it   **C** burn it   **D** eat it

9. Daffodils are a type of ____.
   A bluebell   **B** tulip   **C** jonquil   **D** trumpet

10. The daffodils Dorothy calls stragglers are a bit like people on the edge of a ____.
   A crowd   **B** cliff   **C** body of water   **D** lawn

Kubla Khan

Part A Directions Write the answers to these questions. Use complete
sentences.

1. On what continent would you be most likely to find an "Abyssinian maid?"
Explain your reasoning.

_____

2. On what continent was Kubla Khan's "stately pleasure dome?" Explain how you know.

_____

3. What might Mount Abora and Amara have in common?

_____

Part B Directions Write the correct word from the Word Bank
to complete each sentence.

4. She makes sweet music on her _____.

5. We celebrated our victory with a joyful and noisy
_____.

6. The river wound through a deep, narrow _____
in the mountains.

7. Some insects eat the _____ they find on leaves.

8. I asked _____, or three times, for help.

9. The king created his own _____, a garden filled
with everything he loved.

10. Tara got lost in the _____ passageways.

11. Safe drivers slow down on a(n) _____ road.

12. The broken tree branch lay _____ the trail.

13. Dena _____ onto the horse and galloped off.

14. The unpopular law led to _____ in the streets
as people protested.

15. This writer is _____ a happy outcome.

| **Word Bank** |
| athwart |
| chasm |
| dulcimer |
| honey-dew |
| mazy |
| paradise |
| prophesying |
| sinuous |
| thrice |
| tumult |
| turmoil |
| vaulted |

Pride and Prejudice

Part A Directions Write the answer to these questions. Use complete sentences.

1. Where would you find the context for a word?

_____

2. Why is context important?

_____

Part B Directions Write the correct word from the Word Bank to complete each sentence.

3. His _____ attitude made some people dislike him.

4. My mother's _____ in teaching me to cook is to have me help her sometimes.

5. The howling of the neighbor's dog became very _____.

6. Jane showed _____, or good judgment, in choosing the topic for her paper.

7. While Luke was sick, he found _____ in reading.

8. Lena has read only _____ of the book, so she does not know the whole story.

9. The _____ in the hotel lobby kept me awake.

10. You must be _____ after your long flight.

11. Curt went into _____ describing his new bike.

12. The brave rescuers were _____ admired.

13. My parents gave me a(n) _____ warning about playing near the street.

14. It is _____ to say one thing and do another.

15. The magician never _____ the secrets of his tricks.

Word Bank
design
disclosed
discretion
emphatic
extracts
fatigued
hypocritical
raptures
sarcastic
solace
tiresome
tumult
universally

Pride and Prejudice, continued

Part C Directions Circle the letter of the answer that correctly completes
each sentence.

16. I hear that the property has not been ____.
   A reserve   **B** mean   **C** let   **D** amends

17. She cannot ____ to be there precisely on time.
   A engage   **B** caprice   **C** amends   **D** scrupulous

18. Be very ____ when dividing up the prize money.
   A caprice   **B** mean   **C** scrupulous   **D** conjecturing

19. His ____ condition made him unwilling to fly.
   A vexing   **B** engage   **C** mean   **D** nervous

20. How can I ever make ____ for my blunder?
   A surpassing   **B** amends   **C** engage   **D** let

Part D Directions Match the definition in Column A with the correct word
in Column B. Write the correct letter on each line.

Column A	Column B
_____ **21.** agreed upon as true	**A** reserve
_____ **22.** act of setting up on a solid basis	**B** establishment
_____ **23.** low in quality or value	**C** vexing
_____ **24.** caution in words or actions	**D** caprice
_____ **25.** impulsiveness	**E** circumspection
_____ **26.** wondering; guessing	**F** assemblies
_____ **27.** going beyond	**G** mean
_____ **28.** gatherings of people	**H** acknowledged
_____ **29.** cautious thinking	**I** conjecturing
_____ **30.** annoying; irritating	**J** surpassing

She Walks in Beauty

Part A Directions Circle the letter of the answer that correctly completes each sentence.

1. Add the suffix ____ to the adjective *good* to make a noun meaning "a state of being of a good condition or quality."
    A -less   **B** -y   **C** -ly   **D** -ness

2. Add the suffix ____ to the noun *name* to make an adjective meaning "without a name."
    A -less   **B** -y   **C** -ly   **D** -ness

3. Add the suffix ____ to the noun *star* to make an adjective meaning "full of stars."
    A -less   **B** -y   **C** -ly   **D** -ness

4. Add the suffix ____ to the adjective *soft* to make an adverb meaning "in a soft manner."
    A -less   **B** -y   **C** -ly   **D** -ness

Part B Directions Match the definition in Column A with the correct word or phrase in Column B. Write the correct letter on each line.

Column A	Column B
_____ 5. expressive	**A** impaired
_____ 6. climates	**B** aspect
_____ 7. calmly	**C** eloquent
_____ 8. face	**D** climes
_____ 9. black curl of hair	**E** raven tress
_____ 10. damaged, lessened	**F** serenely

Frankenstein

Part A Directions Write the answers to these questions. Use complete sentences.

1. How does the context of the following passage help explain that *dormant* means *sleeping*? *Some animals sleep when it's cold. In the same way, some plants are dormant in winter.*

_____

2. How does the word *but* in the following passage help you understand the meaning of *uncouth*? *The boys are very well trained, but their friends are uncouth.*

_____

Part B Directions Write the correct word from the Word Bank to complete each sentence.

Word Bank
accumulated
barricade
benevolent
consolation
detestation
diabolically
foliage
immutable
inarticulate
irrevocably
multitude
severity
stature

3. His speech is slurred and _____.

4. The colorful _____ is lovely in autumn.

5. Gravity is a(n) _____ law of physics.

6. I _____ my door to keep my brother out.

7. Piles of mail _____ on her desk while she was gone.

8. Her best friend's visit was a great _____ after she moved to another state.

9. The _____ of the storm frightened us.

10. The villain's evil plan is _____ clever.

11. Caleb is small in _____ but big in spirit.

12. My squeamish brother cannot hide his _____ for spiders.

13. The shelter depends on _____ volunteers who come to help out.

14. The house was _____ damaged by the fire and will have to be torn down.

15. A _____ of fans came to hear the pop star.

Frankenstein, continued

Part C Directions Write the answers to these questions. Use complete
sentences. Your answers should show that you
understand the underlined word.

16. Why might you not choose to climb a <u>precipitous</u> hill?

_____

17. Would it take you longer to run a <u>league</u> or a mile? Explain.

_____

18. How could you help a plant have <u>luxuriant</u> leaves and flowers?

_____

19. Why might a condemned criminal ask for <u>clemency</u>?

_____

20. Would you want to live in an <u>equitable</u> society? Explain.

_____

Part D Directions Match the definition in Column A with the correct word
in Column B. Write the correct letter on each line.

Column A	Column B
_____ **21.** grand	**A** sublime
_____ **22.** hard blow	**B** radiant
_____ **23.** peak	**C** disdain
_____ **24.** having unearthly beauty	**D** comply
_____ **25.** disgusting	**E** abhor
_____ **26.** do as asked	**F** precipices
_____ **27.** hate	**G** imperial
_____ **28.** scorn	**H** odious
_____ **29.** glowing	**I** pinnacle
_____ **30.** steep slopes	**J** concussion

Ozymandias

Part A Directions Circle the letter of the answer that correctly completes each sentence.

1. The word ____ means "a gigantic statue."
   A pediment   **B** colossus   **C** hyperbolic   **D** visceral

2. The words *pedestal, pedestrian,* and *pedal* all relate to the Latin word for ____.
   A head   **B** eye   **C** leg   **D** foot

3. The visor on a hat gets its name from ____.
   A the Latin word *vitis*, meaning "vine"
   B the Old French word *vis*, meaning "face"
   C the Old French word *vice*, meaning "fault"
   D the Latin word *viscosus*, meaning "sticky"

4. Knowing what *colossal* means, you would expect a building called the Colosseum to be ____.
   A very large   **C** a place where gladiators fight
   B in ancient Rome   **D** in ruins

Part B Directions Write the answers to these questions. Use complete sentences. Your answers should show that you understand the underlined word.

5. How would you show that you had <u>colossal</u> strength?

   _____

6. If a photograph shows only your <u>visage</u>, what does it not show?

   _____

7. What might you find on a <u>pedestal</u>?

   _____

8. Where might you go to see some <u>colossal</u> buildings?

   _____

9. Why would a person conceal his or her <u>visage</u>?

   _____

10. If we put someone "on a <u>pedestal</u>," we mean to say that person is very important. Why do people use this expression?

    _____

Ode on a Grecian Urn

Part A Directions Circle the letter of the answer that correctly completes
each sentence.

1. An Attic vase would come from ____.
   A upstairs in your house   **C** Athens
   B a poem   **D** England

2. *Arcady* refers to the ____.
   A city   **B** mountains   **C** country   **D** seaside

Part B Directions Match the definition in Column A with the correct word
in Column B. Write the correct letter on each line.

Column A	Column B
_____ 3. becoming dry	**A** overwrought
_____ 4. hand drums	**B** unravish'd
_____ 5. pure	**C** sylvan
_____ 6. made all over a surface	**D** parching
_____ 7. related to wooded areas	**E** timbrels
_____ 8. overfull	**F** cloy'd

Part C Directions Write the correct word from the Word Bank to
complete each sentence.

9. The animal's ribs showed through its _____.

10. We said a sad _____ to our new friends.

11. The _____ worshippers visited the shrine annually.

12. The path was _____ flat by many hikers.

13. I am _____ to go near that snarling dog.

14. The invading army surrounded the _____.

15. A _____ grazed quietly in the field.

Word Bank
adieu
citadel
flanks
heifer
loth
pious
trodden

In Memoriam

Part A Directions Sometimes words are used in a figurative instead of a literal way. Underline the word or words below that are used in a figurative way. Then write a meaning for the words.

1. "I know transplanted human worth/Will bloom to profit, otherwhere."

_____

2. "I prosper, circled with thy voice . . ."

_____

Part B Directions Match the definition in Column A with the correct word in Column B. Write the correct letter on each line.

	Column A		Column B
_____	**3.** gathers	**A**	otherwhere
_____	**4.** not held back	**B**	void
_____	**5.** empty	**C**	stagnates
_____	**6.** do very well	**D**	wreak
_____	**7.** avenge	**E**	prosper
_____	**8.** laziness	**F**	diffusive
_____	**9.** a small brown bird	**G**	linnet
_____	**10.** elsewhere	**H**	sloth
_____	**11.** permission to act	**I**	nigh
_____	**12.** near	**J**	garners
_____	**13.** lies still and idle	**K**	unfetter'd
_____	**14.** scattered	**L**	wrought
_____	**15.** worked	**M**	licence

My Last Duchess

Directions Read each clue. Then choose the correct word from the Word Bank to complete the puzzle.

Across

- **1.** denied
- **3.** dared
- **5.** thoughtfulness
- **10.** token of love or respect
- **11.** generosity
- **12.** swore
- **13.** taught

Down

- **1.** money and property given for marriage
- **2.** proof
- **4.** silly activity
- **5.** face and expression
- **6.** indeed
- **7.** claim, expectation
- **8.** branch
- **9.** bossy or overbearing
- **11.** loose cloak

Word Bank
avowed
bough
countenance
courtesy
disallowed
dowry
durst
favour
forsooth
lessoned
mantle
munificence
officious
pretence
trifling
warrant

Sonnet 43

Part A Directions Some words have more than one meaning. Use context to write a definition for each boldfaced word below. Then use your own knowledge or a dictionary to write another meaning for the word.

1. ". . . when **feeling** out of sight/For the ends of Being and Ideal Grace."

   _____

2. "I love thee to the **level** of everyday's/Most quiet need . . ."

   _____

3. "I love thee freely, as men strive for **Right** . . ."

   _____

Part B Directions Write the correct word from the Word Bank to complete each sentence.

Word Bank
grace
praise
strive

4. When people _____ my work, I blush with pleasure.

5. She has _____ in both her movements and her attitude.

6. People _____ to reach the goals that are important to them.

Part C Directions Write the answers to these questions. Use complete sentences. Your answers should show that you understand the underlined word.

7. Where have you seen an example of <u>grace</u>?

   _____

8. Why does the poet say people are pure as they "turn from <u>Praise</u>"?

   _____

9. What will you <u>strive</u> to achieve in your life?

   _____

10. How can people have <u>grace</u> in their treatment of others?

    _____

Jane Eyre

Part A Directions Writers sometimes give context clues that are synonyms (words that mean the same) or antonyms (words that mean the opposite) of a difficult word. Each phrase below contains a pair of words that are either synonyms or antonyms. Circle the two words. Then write *synonym* or *antonym* on the line.

1. "... but sitting by him, roused from the nightmare of parting—called to the paradise of union ..." _____

2. "I am a free human being with an independent will ..." _____

3. "I am not talking to you now through the medium of custom, conventionalities, nor even of mortal flesh ..." _____

Part B Directions Write the correct word from the Word Bank to complete each sentence.

4. Her _____ lit up whenever she smiled.

5. A(n) _____ grows beside the garden gate.

6. Rochester became _____ as he spoke with Jane.

7. Jane _____ to pull herself away from Rochester's arms.

8. Miss Ingram's unkind attitude showed her love was a _____.

9. Do you live by _____, or do you do things your own way?

10. Many problems have _____ them during their trip.

11. My mother _____ my participation in sports.

12. The peacock's most noticeable feature is its colorful _____.

13. Jane's _____ is to be married to Rochester.

14. Will his love _____ for all the pain she has suffered?

Word Bank
agitated
atone
befallen
conventionalities
countenance
destiny
farce
laurel
plumage
sanctions
writhed

Jane Eyre, continued

Part C Directions Match the definition in Column A with the correct
word in Column B. Write the correct letter on each
line.

Column A	Column B
_____ **15.** pay a penalty	**A** anguish
_____ **16.** tearing	**B** automaton
_____ **17.** beg	**C** effaced
_____ **18.** honesty	**D** entreat
_____ **19.** rudeness	**E** expiate
_____ **20.** small piece	**F** exultation
_____ **21.** suffering	**G** hasten
_____ **22.** robot	**H** hither
_____ **23.** unknown	**I** incivility
_____ **24.** not believing	**J** incredulous
_____ **25.** breeze	**K** kindred
_____ **26.** comfort	**L** livid
_____ **27.** wiped away	**M** misconstrue
_____ **28.** answered	**N** morsel
_____ **29.** triumph	**O** obscure
_____ **30.** misunderstand	**P** rejoined
_____ **31.** here	**Q** rending
_____ **32.** added	**R** sincerity
_____ **33.** furious	**S** solace
_____ **34.** hurry	**T** subjoined
_____ **35.** relatives	**U** waft

David Copperfield

Part A Directions The etymology of a word is its history. Use a dictionary to answer these questions. Use complete sentences.

1. From what word does the word *sexton* orginally come?

_____

2. What was the meaning of the Latin word from which *humble* comes?

_____

Part B Directions Circle the letter of the answer that correctly completes each sentence.

3. Uriah Heep's ____ are to marry Agnes and to get ahead in the world.
  A visages   **B** aspirations   **C** assertions   **D** suppressions

4. During the governor's speech, the reporter ____ with a question.
  A interposed   **B** engendered   **C** abased   **D** allusion

5. The ____ brought new candles to the church every day.
  A visage   **B** strategems   **C** sexton   **D** malice

6. "Keeping a straight face" is a way to describe the ____ of laughter.
  A suppression   **B** recompense   **C** compulsion   **D** cant

7. The ____ rain forced us to stay indoors all weekend.
  A shambling   **B** engendered   **C** base   **D** unrelenting

8. That dam is ____ a mighty river.
  A compulsion   **B** constraining   **C** unrelenting   **D** detestable

9. His art is very ____, with bold lines and sharp corners.
  A malice   **B** engendered   **C** derisive   **D** angular

10. The camp cook served the same ____ slop every day.
  A temperate   **B** propitiatory   **C** detestable   **D** interposed

11. Uriah's father taught Uriah to ____ himself to gain power over others.
  A recompense   **B** abase   **C** craft   **D** interpose

12. During political campaigns, the public often hears a lot of ____.
  A cant   **B** contortion   **C** allusion   **D** visage

David Copperfield, continued

Part C Directions Write the correct word from the Word Bank
to complete each sentence.

Word Bank
allusion
civilly
condescension
craft
engendered
malice
propitiatory
shambling
temperate
visage

13. The _____ between the two rivals led to a bitter fight.

14. His _____ became still, like a mask, when he heard the news.

15. Her _____ earned her a reputation for improper pride.

16. They danced in a(n) _____ manner, stepping on toes
and bumping into people.

17. She won some games by _____, but she finally got caught.

18. I saw a(n) _____ to *David Copperfield* in a magazine article.

19. David is _____ with Uriah, even when he is very angry.

20. The warm spring days _____ many blossoms on the trees.

21. Speaking _____ during a debate is both polite and wise.

22. Carrie sent a thank-you note as a(n) _____ act after the interview.

Part D Directions Match the definition in Column A with the correct
word in Column B. Write the correct letter on each
line.

Column A

_____ **23.** repeated claims

_____ **24.** force

_____ **25.** tricks; plans

_____ **26.** mocking

_____ **27.** reward

_____ **28.** a claim about something

_____ **29.** wicked; mean

_____ **30.** twisting of the body

Column B

A assertion

B compulsion

C contortion

D derisive

E malevolent

F professions

G recompense

H strategems

Dover Beach

Directions Read each clue. Then choose the correct word
from the Word Bank to complete the puzzle.

Across

1. murky, cloudy

2. shore

4. trembling

7. narrow passage

8. rhythm

9. something that wraps
around

10. in the dark

Down

1. peaceful

3. certainty

5. sad

6. coarse stones left
on the shore

Word Bank
cadence
certitude
darkling
girdle
melancholy
shingles
straits
strand
tranquil
tremulous
turbid

Pied Beauty

Part A Directions Writers sometimes create compound words for a unique effect. For each of the following words from "Pied Beauty," write a brief description in plain language of the image the word calls to mind.

1. *couple-colour* _____

_____

2. *rose-moles* _____

_____

3. *fresh-firecoal* _____

_____

Part B Directions Write the correct word from the Word Bank to complete each sentence.

Word Bank
brinded
counter
dappled
fallow
fickle
plotted
stipple

4. The weather is _____ as the seasons change.

5. The painting had a _____ background created with tiny dots.

6. I saw a _____ cow with a light coat streaked with black hair.

7. Going to the concert is _____ to your plan to stay at home.

8. The tree is _____ with different shades of green

9. My grandmother _____ a quilt by laying out all the pieces on a large table.

10. The _____ will rest and regain nutrients so that crops will grow better there next year.

The Importance of Being Earnest

Part A Directions The prefixes *ir-*, *in-*, and *un-* change the meaning of a word to make it mean the opposite. Add one of these prefixes to each of the following words. Then write a definition for the new word.

1. ____wise   _____

2. ____regular   _____

3. ____significant _____

Part B Directions Match the definition in Column A with the correct word in Column B. Write the correct letter on each line.

	Column A	Column B
_____	**4.** go away	**A** ailment
_____	**5.** nickname	**B** christened
_____	**6.** in the countryside	**C** domesticity
_____	**7.** delightful	**D** entrancing
_____	**8.** totally	**E** indecorous
_____	**9.** illness	**F** invalid
_____	**10.** being alone	**G** metaphysical
_____	**11.** named or renamed	**H** provincial
_____	**12.** abstract	**I** radically
_____	**13.** wrong; unsafe	**J** retire
_____	**14.** someone who is sick	**K** solitude
_____	**15.** improper	**L** unsound

The Importance of Being Earnest, continued

Part C Directions Circle the letter of the answer that correctly completes
each sentence.

16. To be ____for marriage, one must be single.
    A demonstrative   **B** eligible   **C** morbid   **D** notorious

17. His ____ manners disgusted everyone at the party.
    A vulgar   **B** notorious   **C** eligible   **D** demonstrative

18. If Jane had been more ____, her friends would have known what she wanted.
    A notorious   **B** demonstrative   **C** vulgar   **D** eligible

19. The ____ outlaw who robbed five banks was finally caught by the police.
    A eligible   **B** morbid   **C** notorious   **D** demonstrative

20. Running a funeral home might seem to be a ____job.
    A morbid   **B** notorious   **C** demonstrative   **D** vulgar

Part D Directions Write the correct word from the Word Bank
to complete each sentence.

Word Bank
candidly
expurgations
indifferent
irresistible
pulpits
relapse
semi-recumbent
shilly-shallying
speculation
tampers

21. The tired hikers were resting in a _____ position.

22. The candidate spoke _____ about her plans.

23. Her decisive brother will not put up with _____.

24. If someone _____ with the engine, it may not work.

25. Her _____ shortened the program by 30 minutes.

26. After all the _____, nobody guessed the outcome.

27. Just as I was feeling better, I had a _____.

28. The preachers stood in the _____.

29. Jay is _____ about where to go for dinner.

30. The arguments were so _____ that we all had
to agree with the speaker.

To an Athlete Dying Young

Part A Directions Sometimes words are used in a figurative instead of a literal way. Underline the word or words below that are used in a figurative way. Then write a meaning for the words.

1. "... And set you at your threshold down,/Townsman of a stiller town."

_____

2. "Eyes the shady night has shut/Cannot see the record cut ..."

_____

3. "Runners whom renown outran ..."

_____

Part B Directions Match the definition in Column A with the correct word in Column B. Write the correct letter on each line.

Column A	Column B
_____ 4. fame	**A** betimes
_____ 5. support beam in a building	**B** chaired
_____ 6. doorway	**C** garland
_____ 7. early	**D** lintel
_____ 8. crowd	**E** renown
_____ 9. strand of leaves or flowers	**F** rout
_____ 10. carried	**G** threshold

Recessional

Directions Read each clue. Then choose the correct word
from the Word Bank to complete the puzzle.

Across

   1. huge armies
   4. uncivilized
   6. brave
   8. control
   9. in case
   10. stinking
   11. wild with rage or fear

Down

   2. uproar
   3. fragment
   4. high point of land
       jutting into a body
       of water
   5. sorry
   7. display of greatness

Word Bank
contrite
dominion
frantic
headland
heathen
hosts
lest
pomp
reeking
shard
tumult
valiant

"Ah, Are You Digging on My Grave?"

Part A Directions Write the answers to these questions. Use complete sentences.

1. How does the context of the following passage help explain that *tendance* means "taking care"?
Her daily tendance of the garden, including daily watering and good fertilizer, caused it to thrive.

_____

2. Use the context of this verse to write a definition for *fidelity*.
      "Ah, yes! *You* dig upon my grave . . .
      Why flashed it not on me?
      That one true heart was left behind!
      What feeling do we ever find
      To equal among human kind
      A dog's **fidelity**!"

_____

Part B Directions Circle the correct word in the parentheses to complete each sentence.

3. The dog was very (rue / sly) about hiding its bone.

4. My (fidelity / kin) will visit in July.

5. Jason's (kin / tendance) on his ailing grandfather is very loving.

6. A cotton (gin / rue) was used to separate seeds from the cotton.

7. He proves his (fidelity / prodding) by always shopping at the same stores.

8. Louis planted (gin / rue) in his yard.

9. The animal was caught in a (gin / prodding) that was unescapable.

10. The doctor kept (kin / prodding) to try to find out what was wrong with the patient.

The Soldier

Directions In "The Soldier," Rupert Brooke uses a past-tense form for some words that is less common now. Instead of adding *-ed* to form the regular past tense of *bless* and *learn,* he adds a *t* to form *blest* and *learnt.* Look at the following words that have been formed the same way. Write the present-tense verb from which each was formed, as well as the regular past-tense form.

	Present Tense	**Regular Past Tense**
1. leapt	_____	_____
2. dreamt	_____	_____
3. spoilt	_____	_____
4. burnt	_____	_____
5. spilt	_____	_____

Dulce et decorum est

Part A Directions Write the answers to these questions about words in
"Dulce et decorum est." Use complete sentences.

1. The word *guttering* combines *gurgling* and *stuttering.* How does this fit in a description
of a man who seems to be drowning?

_____

2. The light in line 13 is described as "thick." Why is this an unusual or surprising description?

_____

Part B Directions Write the correct word from the Word Bank
to complete each sentence.

Word Bank
ardent
ecstasy
fatigue
flound'ring
froth-   corrupted
guttering
lime
outstripped
sludge
smothering
vile
writhing
zest

3. Kim, a(n) _____ fan, rushed home to see the show.

4. Leslie _____ the other runners to win the race.

5. After the flood, the _____ was ankle-deep in our house.

6. _____ heats quickly when exposed to the air.

7. The rescued swimmer was still _____ after being pulled
to shore.

8. Jim's _____ for travel took him all over the world.

9. The medicine was _____, but it made me feel better.

10. The puppy is _____ to escape the vet's needle.

11. In their _____, the soldiers barely had strength to walk.

12. The poet saw a soldier "_____," or struggling to move.

13. The soldier's _____ lungs could not take in air.

14. In a(n) _____ of excitement, Dom forgot to close the door.

15. Billows of _____ smoke blocked the light and caused breathing problems.

The Second Coming

Part A Directions An allusion is a detail that refers to religion, history, or another work of literature. Briefly explain each allusion below from the poem. Then tell how it adds to the richness of the poem.

1. "Surely the Second Coming is at hand."

_____

2. "When a vast image out of *Spiritus Mundi*/Troubles my sight . . ."

_____

3. "And what rough beast, its hour come round at last,/Slouches towards Bethlehem to be born?"

_____

Part B Directions Match the definition in Column A with the correct word in Column B. Write the correct letter on each line.

	Column A	Column B
_____	**4.** time in which truth or reality becomes known	**A** anarchy
_____	**5.** angry	**B** conviction
_____	**6.** troubled	**C** indignant
_____	**7.** strong belief	**D** intensity
_____	**8.** lawless disorder	**E** revelation
_____	**9.** creeps, sneaks	**F** slouches
_____	**10.** focused strength	**G** vexed

Shooting an Elephant

Part A Directions In his essay, George Orwell uses words from the
Burmese culture about which he writes. Use each of the
words below in a sentence. Your sentence should show
that you understand the word's meaning.

1. raj _____

2. sahib _____

3. mahout _____

Part B Directions Write the correct word from the Word Bank
to complete each sentence.

Word Bank
aimless
altered
caverns
conjurer
dahs
invariably
mahout
metalled
paddy fields
perspective
squeamish
unendurable

4. They grow rice in the _____.

5. The _____ pulled a rabbit from his hat.

6. The _____ wanderer never knew where he would
find himself from one day to the next.

7. A(n) _____ road is easier to travel on than
an unpaved path is.

8. I am not _____ about spiders, but snakes scare me.

9. Sometimes you have to get away from a problem to gain
_____ about it.

10. The terrible heat is almost _____.

11. Tim _____ his voice so his sister would not recognize it.

12. They explored the deep, dark _____ in search of treasure.

13. The people used _____ to cut up the meat.

14. She _____ goes to her grandmother's house every Sunday.

15. The _____ knows how to control the elephant.

Shooting an Elephant, continued

Part C Directions Match the definition in Column A with the correct word in Column B. Write the correct letter on each line.

	Column A		Column B
_____	**16.** cruel ruler	**A**	bazaars
_____	**17.** excuse	**B**	conventionalized
_____	**18.** expected	**C**	despotic
_____	**19.** outdoor markets	**D**	impression
_____	**20.** effect	**E**	intolerable
_____	**21.** bowing low; flat and face down	**F**	municipal
_____	**22.** not bearable	**G**	pretext
_____	**23.** belonging to a town or city	**H**	professed
_____	**24.** replace	**I**	prostrate
_____	**25.** ruling unfairly or cruelly	**J**	sole
_____	**26.** only	**K**	supplant
_____	**27.** claimed	**L**	tyrant

	Column A		Column B
_____	**28.** puzzling	**A**	alternative
_____	**29.** suffering	**B**	baited
_____	**30.** crowding and pushing	**C**	cartridges
_____	**31.** set in one's mind	**D**	crucified
_____	**32.** control and authority	**E**	dominion
_____	**33.** upsetting	**F**	inflicted
_____	**34.** did something to get a reaction	**G**	jostling
_____	**35.** stretched out and pinned down	**H**	magazine
_____	**36.** choice	**I**	perplexing
_____	**37.** caused	**J**	resolute
_____	**38.** frailty due to old age	**K**	senility
_____	**39.** tiny containers for bullets	**L**	stricken
_____	**40.** part of a weapon	**M**	unnerving

British Literature

Shooting an Elephant, continued

Part D Directions Read each clue. Then choose the correct word from the Word Bank to complete the puzzle.

Across

3. weakly
5. frightened; beaten down
10. countless
12. causing damage to
14. small and mean
16. far away
17. run toward something with force
18. maze
19. outraged

Down

1. quick
2. lost in thought
3. uselessness
4. assistant
6. those who abuse their power over others
7. steadily
8. showing dislike
9. leftover part
11. muddy
13. bright
15. roofed

Word Bank	
charge	orderly
cowed	petty
flabbily	preoccupied
futility	ravaging
garish	remnant
innumerable	remote
labyrinth	rhythmically
miry	scandalized
nimble	sneering
oppressors	thatched

The Hollow Men

Part A Directions Write a sentence telling how the poet's use of language in each of the following lines creates an interesting or surprising effect. Make sure your sentence explains what the poet means by the boldfaced word.

1. "Leaning together/**Headpiece** filled with straw. Alas!"

_____

2. "Let me also wear/Such deliberate disguises/Rat's coat, **crowskin,** crossed staves/In a field . . ."

_____

3. "This is the dead land/This is **cactus** land . . ."

_____

Part B Directions Circle the correct word in the parentheses to complete each sentence.

4. The (multifoliate / potency) of this vitamin has increased.

5. The scarecrow hangs on two (descents / staves).

6. The (paralysed / tumid) lake threatened to burst the dam.

7. Do you have any (conception / potency) of what you will do after graduation?

8. This garden has many (multifoliate / perpetual) plants.

9. I have a(n) (essence / perpetual) calendar that can be used year after year.

10. You must (grope / spasm) in the dark to find the secret opening.

11. A (conception / spasm) of fear ran through her as the deer bolted in front of the car.

12. The (descent / essence) from the mountain's summit was very dangerous.

13. The (essence / staves) of this report can be found in the summary.

14. The professor ignored the students' (conception / supplication) for more time.

15. Ben was (paralysed / tumid) with indecision.

The Duchess and the Jeweller

Part A Directions Match the description in Column A with the correct London place name in Column B. Write the correct letter on each line.

Column A	Column B
_____ **1.** Oliver Bacon has suits made here	**A** Bond Street
	B Hatton Garden
_____ **2.** Bacon's jewelry shop is located here	**C** Savile Row
_____ **3.** A famous jewelry district	

Part B Directions Circle the letter of the answer that correctly completes each sentence.

4. The cowboy had a saddlebag made of ____.
   A flounces   **B** iridescences   **C** sideboard   **D** shagreen

5. The host served caviar and ____ at the dinner party.
   A trellises   **B** pâté de foie gras   **C** tiaras   **D** ferret

6. The ____ moon lights the night sky.
   A compressed   **B** waggled   **C** lustrous   **D** astute

7. This museum has some beautiful ____ in its "Jewelry Through the Ages" exhibit.
   A waistcoats   **B** flounces   **C** ducal coronets   **D** trellises

8. A ____ was small enough to be pulled by only one horse.
   A hansom cab   **B** guinea   **C** prestige   **D** villa

9. John's costume was perfect, down to the spotless white ____ on his shoes.
   A parasols   **B** spats   **C** grating   **D** mantelpieces

10. Kelly added ____ to her special pasta sauce.
   A spats   **B** truffles   **C** iridescences   **D** homage

11. The ballgown was made of white ____.
   A ferret   **B** guinea   **C** shagreen   **D** taffeta

The Duchess and the Jeweller, continued

Part C Directions Match the definition in Column A with the correct word in Column B. Write the correct letter on each line.

	Column A		Column B
_____	**12.** a dainty umbrella	**A**	acknowledged
_____	**13.** marked with dimples	**B**	cincture
_____	**14.** British unit of money	**C**	compressed
_____	**15.** frames for supporting plants	**D**	dimpling
_____	**16.** furniture used for storage	**E**	guinea
_____	**17.** a sash	**F**	laden
_____	**18.** waved back and forth	**G**	parasol
_____	**19.** full	**H**	queried
_____	**20.** pressed together tightly	**I**	sideboard
_____	**21.** recognized	**J**	trellises
_____	**22.** asked	**K**	waggled
_____	**23.** folding case	**L**	wallet

	Column A		Column B
_____	**24.** windows that curve outward	**A**	bays
_____	**25.** narrow passageways	**B**	discreet
_____	**26.** fancy vests	**C**	ferret
_____	**27.** honor	**D**	figured
_____	**28.** small weasel-like animal	**E**	grating
_____	**29.** respectfully	**F**	hide
_____	**30.** not calling attention to itself	**G**	homage
_____	**31.** place in life; destiny	**H**	lot
_____	**32.** animal skin; leather	**I**	obsequiously
_____	**33.** richly decorated or trimmed	**J**	straits
_____	**34.** a metal screen over an opening	**K**	tiaras
_____	**35.** women's jeweled headbands	**L**	waistcoats

British Literature

The Duchess and the Jeweller, continued

Part D Directions Write the correct word from the Word Bank
to complete each sentence.

36. The _____ boy darted in and out
among the crowds.

37. The wave left seaweed on the sand as it _____.

38. The artist had a(n) _____ to create a statue
for the new park.

39. The medal on his uniform is a mark of great _____.

40. Please _____ the letter from this envelope for me.

41. Julie _____ the engine and put it back together
faster than either of her brothers.

42. The _____ brass doorknobs gleamed.

43. If we ever go to Italy, we hope to stay in a(n) _____
in the country.

44. The _____ politician gave clever answers to avoid
saying anything unpopular.

45. The way she _____ made people wonder
what secret she was keeping.

Word Bank
astute
burnished
commission
dismantled
extract
leered
lissome
prestige
subsided
villa

A Cup of Tea

Part A Directions Underline the context clues in the following sentences.
Then define each boldfaced word in your own words.

1. The **languid** woman, limp and still, barely had strength to hold her teacup.

   _____

2. Jane will ask the **milliner** to make a special hat for the occasion.

   _____

Part B Directions Match the definition in Column A with the correct
word in Column B. Write the correct letter on each
line.

	Column A	Column B
_____	**3.** very pleased	**A** bodice
_____	**4.** varnish	**B** exquisitely
_____	**5.** unusual; not refined	**C** extraordinary
_____	**6.** healthful; giving strength	**D** fortunate
_____	**7.** top portion of a dress	**E** frightfully
_____	**8.** dare	**F** gratified
_____	**9.** strange and amazing	**G** guinea
_____	**10.** done without thought	**H** impulsively
_____	**11.** going quickly	**I** lacquer
_____	**12.** British unit of money	**J** languor
_____	**13.** lucky; wealthy	**K** mantelpiece
_____	**14.** hateful	**L** milliner
_____	**15.** beam above a fireplace	**M** nourishing
_____	**16.** very	**N** odious
_____	**17.** fit to be seen	**O** presentable
_____	**18.** perfectly	**P** quaint
_____	**19.** relaxation	**Q** skimming
_____	**20.** person who makes hats	**R** venture

A Cup of Tea, continued

Part C Directions Read each clue. Then choose the correct word from the Word Bank to complete the puzzle.

Across

2. limp
4. British unit of money
6. strange; uncommon
7. not calling attention to itself
8. comfortable
9. accept as true
13. surprised; scared
14. awful
15. tiny
16. huge
17. British slang for *darling*

Down

1. politely
3. a type of flowering plant
4. tried to tempt
5. ate greedily
10. angel
11. lacking energy
12. very pleased

Word Bank	
acknowledge	immense
cherub	languid
comfy	listless
devoured	minute
discreet	plied
duck	pound
exotic	startled
geranium	tactfully
gratified	vile

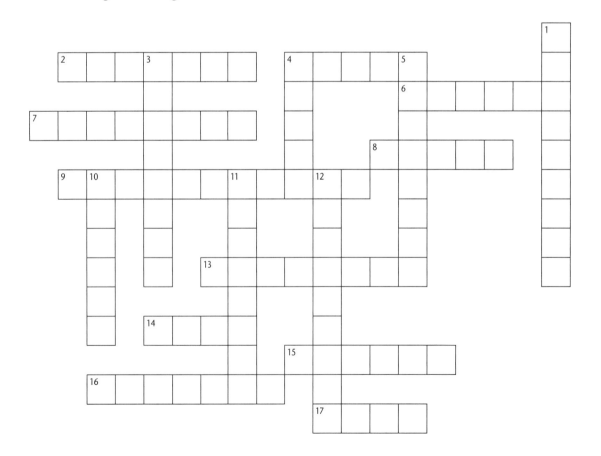

Musée des Beaux Arts

Part A Directions Writers use opposite words and phrases to create startling contrasts. Underline the opposite ideas in each line. Then write a sentence about the contrast they show.

1. "... when the aged are reverently, passionately waiting/ ... there always must be/ Children who did not especially want it to happen ..."

   _____

2. "... even the dreadful martyrdom must run its course/ ... Where the dogs go on with their doggy life ...".

   _____

Part B Directions Circle the letter of the answer that correctly completes each sentence.

3. The _____ is ready for the spring planting.
   A martyrdom   **B** Icarus   **C** ship   **D** ploughman

4. In awe, Eliza bowed _____ as the queen passed by.
   A reverently   **B** sadly   **C** leisurely   **D** dully

5. They strolled _____ around the lake every day of their vacation.
   A wrongly   **B** doggily   **C** leisurely   **D** cruelly

6. In some places, people suffer _____ for their beliefs.
   A martyrdom   **B** miracles   **C** birth   **D** skating

Part C Directions Use each word in a sentence.

7. leisurely _____

8. martyrdom _____

9. ploughman _____

10. reverently _____

What I Expected

Part A Directions Sometimes words are used in a figurative instead of a literal way. Underline the word or words below that are used in a figurative way. Then write a meaning for the words.

1. "... the gradual day/Weakening the will/Leaking the brightness away"

_____

2. "The pulverous grief/Melting the bones with pity"

_____

3. "Some final innocence/ ... That, hanging solid,/Would dangle through all/ Like the created poem ..."

_____

Part B Directions Circle the letter of the answer that correctly completes each sentence.

4. The meal of a carrot and a cup of water was _____.
   A continual   **B** exempt   **C** unsubstantial   **D** pulverous

5. The _____ computer files contained a virus.
   A corrupt   **B** unsubstantial   **C** facet   **D** continue

6. The _____ diamond sparkled in the light.
   A exempt   **B** faceted   **C** pulverous   **D** continual

7. The roads undergo _____ repairs from April until November.
   A exempt   **B** faceted   **C** unsubstantial   **D** continual

8. Ground cinnamon is the _____ form of cinnamon sticks.
   A continual   **B** unsubstantial   **C** pulverous   **D** faceted

9. Some students were _____ from the exam because they did special projects instead.
   A exempt   **B** corrupt   **C** continual   **D** pulverous

10. The _____ chanting from the other team's fans was very annoying.
   A pulverous   **B** unsubstantial   **C** continual   **D** exempt

Blood, Toil, Tears and Sweat

Directions Read each clue. Then choose the correct word
from the Word Bank to complete the puzzle.

Across

2. exceeded
7. excuse
8. assignment
9. terrible
10. stubborn or fixed
12. rebuilding
13. optimism; good spirits
14. task

Down

1. list
3. follow to the end
4. firmness of mind
5. making one sorry
or sad
6. beginning
7. ending until
a later time
11. hardness

Word Bank	
adjournment	preliminary
allowance	prosecute
buoyancy	reconstruction
catalogue	resolve
commission	rigour
grievous	surpassed
inflexible	undertaking
lamentable	

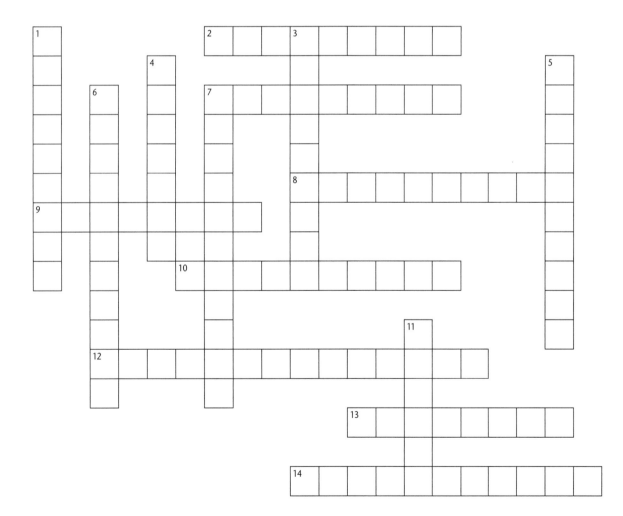

Do Not Go Gentle into That Good Night

Part A Directions Sometimes words are used in a figurative instead of a literal way. Underline the word or words below that are used in a figurative way. Then write a meaning for the words.

1. "Old age should burn and rave at close of day"

_____

2. "Their frail deeds might have danced in a green bay"

_____

3. "Blind eyes could blaze like meteors"

_____

Part B Directions Circle the letter of the answer that correctly completes each sentence.

4. He was in _____ condition after the surgery.
  A rave   **B** forked   **C** wise   **D** grave

5. Did you hear him _____ about his crazy dream?
  A grave   **B** rave   **C** bless   **D** fork

6. Fighting in a war is a very _____ situation.
  A frail   **B** grave   **C** rave   **D** forked

7. The lightning _____ and struck several trees.
  A raved   **B** graved   **C** forked   **D** died

Part C Directions Use each word in a sentence.

8. forked _____

9. grave _____

10. rave _____

British Literature

The Horses

Part A Directions Writers sometimes create compound words for a
unique effect. For each of the following words from
"The Horses," write a brief description in plain
language of the image the word calls to mind.

1. *frost-making* _____

_____

2. *megalith-still* _____

_____

Part B Directions Circle the correct word in the parentheses to complete
each sentence.

3. The (din / dregs) made it impossible for us to have a conversation.

4. Terry saw a (megalith / moorline) when he visited the ruins of the ancient temple.

5. The animals began (kindling / stirring) when the rooster crowed.

6. The (draped / tortuous) knot will be difficult to untie.

7. He stood on the (din / moor-ridge) to view the horses.

8. Jess took lots of pictures so that her memory of the trip would (endure / kindle).

9. The (dregs / moorlines) of tea in the bottom of the cup are bitter

10. The table was (draped / tortuous) in patriotic colors.

A Shocking Accident

Part A Directions   Suffixes change the meaning of words, often changing them into a different part of speech. Write the base word and the suffix for each word below. Then write the meaning of each word based on your knowledge of each word part. (You may use a dictionary if you are unsure.)

1. commiseration _____

_____

2. amusement _____

_____

Part B Directions   Circle the correct word in the parentheses to complete each sentence.

3. Only push this button as a last (discourse / resort)

4. Most of the runners were (flagging / recounting) by the end of the race.

5. The appearance of the strange lights was (inevitably / inexplicable).

6. Though Jane was nervous, she remained (composed / obscure) during the interview.

7. When I think of Hawaii, I (expel / visualize) lovely beaches and blue waves.

8. Dave's (apprehension / commiseration) about public speaking has never gone away.

9. Children are (distinguished / intrinsically) imaginative.

10. The (obscure / distinguished) speaker shared the story of her amazing success.

11. The tasteless joke showed his (anti-climax / callousness) about the problem.

12. The (disclosure / resort) of the company's financial problems caused panic.

13. The famous poet also wrote one (obscure / ricochetted) play that did not do well.

14. Leslie (appeased / embarked) on her career by writing for a small newspaper.

15. Storytelling is the art of (flagging / recounting) interesting tales.

A Shocking Accident, continued

Part C Directions Match the definition in Column A with the term in
Column B. Write the correct letter on each line.

Column A

_____ **16.** unavoidably

_____ **17.** position or job

_____ **18.** government records office

_____ **19.** slum

_____ **20.** letdown

_____ **21.** confusion

_____ **22.** fit of shaking

_____ **23.** a branch of math dealing with triangles

_____ **24.** force out

_____ **25.** bounced

Column B

A anti-climax

B capacity

C convulsion

D expel

E inevitably

F perplexity

G registry-office

H ricochetted

I tenement

J trigonometry

Part D Directions Write the correct word from the Word Bank to
complete each sentence.

26. Dena _____ a lot after her cat ran away.

27. Riding bikes on busy sidewalks is a _____.

28. Her rude comments about the food were very _____.

29. Students in the higher _____ take more classes.

30. Her _____ is about her research into ancient cultures.

31. The _____ man was lonely without his wife.

32. I will talk to the _____ of the inn about getting
an extra blanket.

33. You will learn how to calculate averages in _____ class.

34. Lincoln's three-minute Gettysburg Address is famous for its
_____.

35. The bottle of milk _____ the cranky baby.

Word Bank
appeased
brevity
brooded
forms
insensitive
menace
proprietor
statistics
thesis
widowed

Not Waving but Drowning

Part A Directions Match the British word in Column A with the more common American word in Column B. Write the correct letter on each line. (One British word comes from a previous selection. If you do not remember it, use the process of elimination to recall it.)

Column A	Column B
_____ **1.** larking	**A** fellow
_____ **2.** chap	**B** darling
_____ **3.** duck	**C** joking

Part B Directions Write the meaning of the word in your own words.

4. larking

_____

Part C Directions Use the word in a sentence.

5. larking

_____

Beat the Blues with Brian

Directions Read each clue. Then choose the correct word
from the Word Bank to complete the puzzle.

Across

- **4.** sniffing noisily
- **8.** embarrassment
- **10.** confusion
- **11.** energetic
- **13.** man
- **14.** set of four
- **15.** a Latin grammatical term
- **19.** awful
- **20.** out of contact with reality
- **21.** urging or encouraging

Down

- **1.** severe headache
- **2.** hissing
- **3.** illnesses
- **5.** called up
- **6.** fed up or annoyed
- **7.** dreamlike, strange
- **9.** opening remark
- **12.** wild
- **16.** insult
- **17.** very small
- **18.** mix

Word Bank

ablative absolute	migraine
affront	mortification
bloke	psychotic
conjured	quartet
disarray	raucous
exasperated	sibilant
exhortation	snuffling
gambit	surreal
grisly	titchy
maladies	vigorous
	welter

Araby

Part A Directions Identify the root of each word. Write two more words
with the same root. Use a dictionary if you need help.

1. amiability

_____

2. odorous

_____

3. liberated

_____

Part B Directions Circle the correct word in the parentheses to complete
each sentence.

4. Doing the same things every day can be (hostile / monotonous).

5. The (indistinct / flaring) party was noisy and crowded.

6. The message that he left was (indistinct / odorous) and hard to hear.

7. Dennis wants to find a new (salver / tenant) to rent the apartment.

8. The (pious / ruinous) house will be torn down next week.

9. Everyone was in a(n) (improvised / sombre) mood after the difficult test.

10. Leana shrugged (intolerably / resignedly) when she was told about the three-hour delay.

Araby, continued

Part C Directions   Match the definition in Column A with the word in Column B. Write the correct letter on each line.

Column A	Column B
_____ **11.** parted	**A** derided
_____ **12.** unbearable	**B** diverged
_____ **13.** weak	**C** feeble
_____ **14.** a series of challenges	**D** florin
_____ **15.** delighted	**E** gantlet
_____ **16.** mocked	**F** girdled
_____ **17.** fills	**G** improvised
_____ **18.** began to doubt	**H** intolerable
_____ **19.** freed	**I** liberated
_____ **20.** china	**J** luxuriated
_____ **21.** soaked	**K** misgave
_____ **22.** surrounded	**L** murmured
_____ **23.** spoke in low tones	**M** pervades
_____ **24.** a silver coin	**N** porcelain
_____ **25.** set up for temporary use	**O** sodden

Araby, continued

Part D Directions Read each clue. Then choose the correct word
from the Word Bank to complete the puzzle.

Across

1. bottom of a window frame
3. rubbed raw; became irritated
5. serving dish
6. smelly
8. unfriendly
9. call or command
12. not having strong emotions
14. chants or repeated calls
16. talkative
17. boring
18. foolish pride

Down

2. wipe out
3. generous
4. came together
7. endless or constant
9. tried hard
10. friendliness
11. intrude
13. great pain
15. religious

Word Bank	
amiability	incessant
anguish	litanies
annihilate	odorous
chafed	pious
charitable	salver
converged	sash
garrulous	strove
hostile	summons
imperturbable	tedious
impinge	vanity

Next Term We'll Mash You

Part A Directions Write one synonym and one antonym for each word.
Use a thesaurus if you need help.

	Synonym	**Antonym**
1. delicate	_____	_____
2. expensive	_____	_____

Part B Directions Circle the letter of the answer that correctly completes
each sentence.

3. People should speak in _____ tones in a library.
  A indulgent   **B** mutilated   **C** dappled   **D** subdued

4. Charles will be in the third _____ in his new school.
  A form   **B** din   **C** quid   **D** homespun

5. Jo will get new _____ to wear at camp.
  A tarmacs   **B** pavilions   **C** prospectuses   **D** plimsolls

6. Chris was very _____ about how late his friends arrived.
  A homespun   **B** indulgent   **C** inaccessible   **D** preparatory

7. A helium balloon _____, or shrinks, when taken into cold temperatures.
  A extinguishes   **B** contracts   **C** mutilates   **D** subdues

8. I could not hear the announcement because of the _____ in the waiting room.
  A din   **B** quid   **C** form   **D** au pair

9. I pulled what was left of my letter out of the _____ envelope.
  A amiable   **B** subdued   **C** kaleidoscopic   **D** mutilated

10. Cade read through all the _____ before choosing which schools to visit.
  A tarmac   **B** prospectuses   **C** condescension   **D** repartee

Next Term We'll Mash You, continued

Part C Directions Write the correct word from the Word Bank
to complete each sentence.

11. The national _____ team from India is undefeated.

12. The students were distracted by their _____ of spring break.

13. Baking soda is useful for _____ some kinds of kitchen fires.

14. The _____ rain pounded down.

15. As a(n) _____, Nadia takes care of children and helps
    around the house.

16. In the event of rain, the picnic will be moved into the _____.

17. The colorful flashing lights in the arcade create a _____ effect.

18. Under the trees, the grass was _____ with sunlight.

19. _____ does not contribute to good teamwork.

20. The workers heaved the _____ old armchair into the junk bin.

Word Bank

anticipation
au pair
condescension
cricket
dappled
extinguishing
kaleidoscopic
mangy
pavilion
torrential

Part D Directions Match the definition in Column A with the word in
Column B. Write the correct letter on each line.

Column A	Column B
_____ 21. unreachable	**A** amiable
_____ 22. plain	**B** geniality
_____ 23. teasing talk	**C** haggard
_____ 24. allowed	**D** homespun
_____ 25. pavement	**E** inaccessible
_____ 26. not spoiled	**F** licensed
_____ 27. tired	**G** preparatory
_____ 28. friendly	**H** repartee
_____ 29. friendliness	**I** tarmac
_____ 30. getting ready for something	**J** untainted

A Mild Attack of Locusts

Part A Directions Literature from the British dominions often tells of ways of life very different from what most Americans know. Doris Lessing uses words that are vivid and precise to describe life on an African farm. Write a sentence about the story with each of the following words. Make sure the context of your sentence shows that you understand the meaning of the word.

1. veldt _____

_____

2. mealies _____

_____

3. hoppers _____

_____

Part B Directions Circle the correct word in the parentheses to complete each sentence.

4. He (hoisted / stoked) a huge kettle onto the stove.

5. The bike was (mangled / pelting) after Dad backed into it with the car.

6. The national park was (devastated / submerged) by the wildfire.

7. Kara spoke (loathsome / emphatically) about the importance of volunteering.

8. Hail was (eliminating / pelting) the town for half an hour.

9. The sticky honey (clotted / serrated) the mouth of the jar.

10. Hurricanes and tornadoes are (haggard / ruinous) when they strike.

11. They (distorted / stoked) the fire by adding more kindling to it.

12. The locusts' wings created a (ceaseless / disapproving) buzz on the farm.

A Mild Attack of Locusts, continued

Part C Directions Write the correct word from the Word Bank
to complete each sentence.

Word Bank
acrid
compound
eliminating
foliage
homestead
imminent
maneuvering
oppressive
perverted
plague
roused
submerged
surging

13. Jake is _____ sugary snacks from his diet.

14. A _____ struck London in the 1600s, killing
100,000 people.

15. The heat was so _____ that we barely had energy to walk.

16. The chemical gave off _____ fumes that made
our eyes water.

17. The settlers traveled west to claim land for a(n) _____.

18. Justice is _____ if a poor person cannot get legal help.

19. The autumn _____ is wonderfully colorful in New England.

20. The crowds were _____ by Martin Luther King's speeches.

21. Lydia is _____ through the crowded hallway to get to class.

22. The workers' _____ included houses, a school, and a clinic.

23. The sunken ship has been _____ for a hundred years.

24. The waves were _____ as the tropical storm approached.

25. Spring is _____ when the days start to get longer.

Part D Directions Match the definition in Column A with the correct word
in Column B. Write the correct letter on each line.

Column A	Column B
_____ 26. steep slope separating level surfaces	**A** clamor
_____ 27. toothed on the edge	**B** escarpment
_____ 28. not able to be fixed	**C** exasperating
_____ 29. loud, continuous noise	**D** haggard
_____ 30. tired	**E** irremediable
_____ 31. echoing	**F** loathsome
_____ 32. dry grassland	**G** myriads
_____ 33. annoying	**H** reverberating
_____ 34. disgusting	**I** serrated
_____ 35. uncountable numbers	**J** veldt

Games at Twilight

Part A Directions In "Games at Twilight," Anita Desai includes descriptions of plants. These descriptions give readers a sense for the setting. For each plant, write a description of your own, using information from the selection, your own prior knowledge, or other resources.

1. bougainvillea _____

_____

2. eucalyptus _____

_____

Part B Directions Write the correct word from the Word Bank to complete each sentence.

	Word Bank
	clinched
	contemplated
	dejectedly
	exposed
	jubilation
	lavishly
	reappearance
	roused
	sidled
	spiritedly

3. The team sat _____ in the locker room after losing the game.

4. Cory can speak _____ about any cause that she really believes in.

5. Learning that my favorite author would be signing autographs _____ my decision to go to the conference.

6. The children danced with _____ when the rain was finally over.

7. We were _____ to take action by the stirring speech.

8. Because he forgot his jacket, Michael was _____ to the cold.

9. Calvin _____ the meaning of the thought-provoking book he had read.

10. We _____ over to the refreshment table.

11. The _____ of a long-absent character in a TV show is a surprise.

12. She decorated her bedroom _____, using rich colors and lots of artwork.

Games at Twilight, continued

Part C Directions Match the definition in Column A with the correct
word in Column B. Write the correct letter on each line

	Column A	Column B
_____	**13.** came between	**A** compost
_____	**14.** roofed, open porch	**B** definable
_____	**15.** fight or conflict	**C** fray
_____	**16.** glory	**D** hirsute
_____	**17.** able to be explained	**E** intervened
_____	**18.** blocked by mucus	**F** laurels
_____	**19.** decayed plant matter	**G** livid
_____	**20.** hairy	**H** melancholy
_____	**21.** made breathing hard	**I** phlegm-obstructed
_____	**22.** very sad	**J** skittering
_____	**23.** bruised	**K** stifled
_____	**24.** skipping quickly	**L** veranda

	Column A	Column B
_____	**25.** gloomy, like a funeral	**A** confinement
_____	**26.** repeated lines in a song or poem	**B** formation
_____	**27.** captivity	**C** funereal
_____	**28.** refreshingly good	**D** ignominy
_____	**29.** quenching	**E** intoxicating
_____	**30.** arrangement	**F** legitimate
_____	**31.** permitted	**G** magenta
_____	**32.** shame	**H** mortuary
_____	**33.** in a way that shows dislike	**I** refrain
_____	**34.** purplish red	**J** slaking
_____	**35.** funeral home	**K** superciliously

Games at Twilight, continued

Part D Directions Read each clue. Then choose the correct word
from the Word Bank to complete the puzzle.

Across

1. unimportance
6. boldness
8. crazy
10. very dry
12. in a comforting way
14. without feeling
16. no longer used
18. not definite
19. half-circle
20. harshly

Down

2. clothing worn by Hindu women
3. advising
4. angry, swollen look
5. shaking
7. kept busy
9. sad
11. gloomy, like a tomb
13. chanting
15. stubborn
17. avoid

Word Bank

arc	lugubrious
arid	maniacal
benumbed	occupied
counselling	reassuringly
defunct	sari
dogged	sepulchral
elude	stridently
insignificance	temerity
intoning	vague
lividity	vibrations

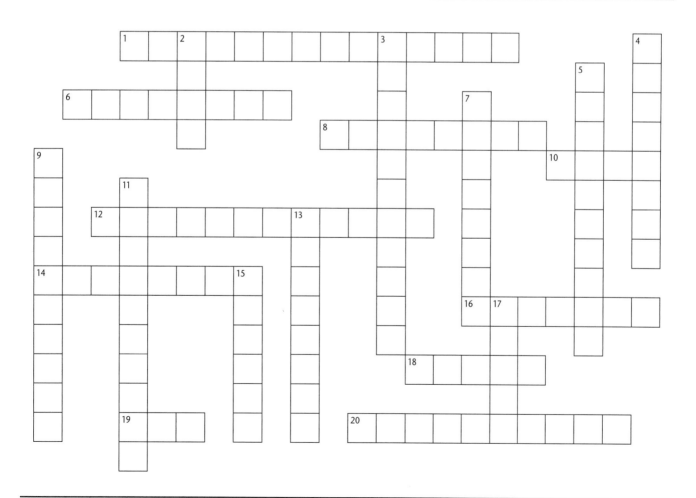

Omeros

Part A Directions In *Omeros,* Derek Walcott uses terms that refer to fishing—the profession of the main characters. Write a sentence with each of the following fishing-related words. Make sure the context of your sentence shows that you understand the meaning of the word.

1. gunwale _____

_____

2. seine _____

_____

Part B Directions Match the definition in Column A with the word in Column B. Write the correct letter on each line.

Column A	Column B
_____ **3.** units for measuring water depth	**A** ancestral
_____ **4.** inherited	**B** bracketed
_____ **5.** large, weighted fishing net	**C** compère
_____ **6.** expression of sympathy	**D** condolence
_____ **7.** anger or irritation	**E** fathoms
_____ **8.** chiseled	**F** gauging
_____ **9.** trench	**G** gunwale
_____ **10.** ritual or custom	**H** incised
_____ **11.** measuring	**I** rite
_____ **12.** companion	**J** seine
_____ **13.** upper edge of the side of a boat	**K** swift
_____ **14.** attached	**L** trough
_____ **15.** a bird like a swallow	**M** vexation